MW01204987

QuickBooks© -
The Easy Way

By Donna L. MacMillan

QuickBooks - The Easy Way
    By Donna L. MacMillan

First Edition

ISBN: 978-1441434401

Trademarks: All names and terms included in this book that
are known to the author to be trademarks have been
capitalized as appropriate. QuickBooks is a registered
trademark of Intuit, Inc.

Disclaimer: While every effort has been made to make this
book as complete and accurate as possible, no warranty is
implied and the information is provided on an "as is basis".
The author and publisher has neither liability nor
responsibility to any person or entity with respect to any
loss or damages resulting from the information contained in
this book.

Table of Contents

Introduction   1

Bookkeeping   4

About The Author   11

Where to Begin   16

Choosing Your Tools   22

Which QuickBooks Version   31
    Is Right For You?

All The Accounting A   40
    Business Owner Needs
    to Know

Setting Up Your Books   62

Setting Up Users   93

Setting Up Preferences   110

Setting Up Items   149

Other Lists To Consider   176

Entering Open Balances   200

Adding Customers   220

Adding Vendors   229

What Is Next?   234

Ready To Use Your   248
Database

Mission Accomplished   267

Appendix A: 269
    New Features in 2011

Appendix B: 277
    List of QuickBooks File Extensions

Appendix C: *281*
      Subcontractor vs an Employee

Appendix D: *286*
      Information to Gather

Appendix E: *289*
      Chart of Accounts Numbering
      Schemes & Parent vs Sub Accounts

Introduction

You have a great idea for a product or service that you know will make you the next multi-millionaire. Your family and friends either think you are brilliant or crazy. Perhaps you are not happy with your current employer or career and desire more control of your work and career. After all if you are like me, there is no better boss to work for than yourself. So how can you fail? Wrong question! The question you should be asking is how can I succeed?

One of the key ingredients of creating a successful business is to understand the ins and outs of managing your money.

A good bookkeeping system is the only way to reach this goal.

Or perhaps your business is offering bookkeeping services to local businesses. Each business has unique needs and you need to be able to setup or reconfigure their QuickBooks data file to satisfy their needs. To be a business person's "hero" and thus keep their continuing business and gain valuable references and referrals, your job includes not only posting transactions, but getting all you can out of QuickBooks, providing accurate, current and valuable data for your client. Not to mention that your own books should be providing you with the same accurate, current and valuable data.

Bookkeeping

What does the term bookkeeping mean to you? Most people see it as writing checks, paying bills and issuing invoices to their clients. Bookkeeping is much more then these functions. Bookkeeping is the process of recording all the money transactions that occur in the day to day running of a business accurately and lawfully.

Many governmental agencies and other associations have developed procedures, laws and rules that determine how a business's financial transactions can be recorded and what standard reports are necessary. Today's business owner has to know the basics of these requirements to stay in good standing.

A good bookkeeping system provides and summarizes the information necessary for report preparations that detail the business's financial information for internal and external review and in the preparation of tax returns.

Bookkeeping provides two kinds of information. One is the current value or equity of a business and the second is the profit or loss that took place over a specific period of time. You the business owner, as well as banks, investors, government agencies and credit grantors all need the use of this information. The business owner needs to see from where the money is coming and where it is being spent as well as whether the business is actually making a profit. No sense in being in business if you are not planning on making a profit.

Investors require information to interpret the results of business operations and make future decisions on either holding or increasing their investments.

Banks and other credit grantors need to have access to information that allows them to make sound decisions on a business's credit worthiness.

And the governmental agencies require you to have accurate and up to date financial records to file your tax returns.

Bookkeeping is really quite an ancient practice within commercial businesses. Found within the ruins of Babylon are records of commercial contracts and accounts. Also the farms and estates of ancient Greece and Rome used accounts to track their financial records. It was with the development of commercial republics in Italy that we first see the double-entry method of bookkeeping being used. It was in the 15th century in various cities within

Italy that bookkeeping instruction manuals appeared.

When the Industrial Revolution of the late 18th and early 19th centuries arrived there was an important stimulus towards bookkeeping. With the rise of manufacturing, trading, shipping and the services associated with these businesses accurate records became a real necessity. If you follow the historic growth of commercial, industrial and government growth you will see a close tie to the growth of bookkeeping systems. As we reached towards global expansion we required more sophisticated means of making financial decisions which required more advanced ways of accumulating, presenting and examining financial information. As more information was needed by both business owners and the people they dealt with as well as increased governmental requirements, the demand for bookkeepers increased.

Basic bookkeeping procedures have not changed much through the centuries, however the way the work is accomplished certainly has. With the arrival of computers the ability to record and analyze more information in less time has brought the business owner an opportunity to reach the goal of having a true understanding of the effects of the business's financial transactions and decisions.

Finally bookkeeping procedures can be broken down into two types. The recording of daily transactions with a journal and the accumulation of these entries into individual accounts called ledgers. From the ledgers, reports such as balance sheets and income (or profit and loss) statements can be prepared.

Setting up your QuickBooks database correctly from the start will allow you use all the tools you need to obtain current, accurate and valuable financial information easy and consistently.

About The Author

My name is Donna MacMillan and it has been my passion over many years to work with business owners during the all important startup and growth phases. I am a certified consultant and trainer who has over 30 years of experience setting up bookkeeping systems which includes the important decisions of what software program to purchase, as well as setting up a business's system right the first time, overseeing the system as the business grows and providing ongoing training for both the business owner and their staff.

Because I have consulted with many startups I know what is needed from the start to enable a business owner to work towards having a well defined accounting system. One that will work not just at the beginning of the business but will be a foundation to build upon as the business grows.

I have completed and have been Advanced Certified in the QuickBooks product line including Intuit Enterprise Solutions and provide consulting and custom training for their extensive family of accounting software products. I use QuickBooks in my business and for my clients. I continue to increase my knowledge in this area to bring better training to my clients.

As the author and web developer of http:// bookkeepingrus.com/blog, a web site dedicated to the education of business owners and bookkeepers, I write free articles outlining how-to's for QuickBooks products as well as articles on running a small business, bookkeeping tips, career advice and much more. I encourage you to visit to see what it's all about and to come back often.

My clients are found within a wide range of industries such as the construction trades including custom home builders, designers and architects, as well as other industries such as professional services, artists and art galleries, manufacturing, wholesalers and non-profits.

It is my dream to educate both new and existing business owners to the importance of keeping a good set of books. Bookkeeping is the key ingredient a business owner needs but it is often put on the back burner. I bring my years of experience, education and knowledge to you, the business owner, so that you may reach your dreams of success. I sincerely believe you will get a great deal of understanding of your business's financial needs and status within these pages. And it all starts with a properly set up set of books!

Where To Begin

If you are just starting your business now is the time to decide how and who will be doing your bookkeeping. If you have already been in business for a while then maybe you need to rethink your bookkeeping processes. With both of these scenarios in mind here are a few suggestions to get you on your way.

The first decision revolves around the "who" question. Will it be or is it already you, a family member or friend who will or is performing these functions. For most people this is the usual situation because most new business owners do not understand the effect a good bookkeeping system can have on the success of their business. The thought process is usually "I can write checks and prepare invoices, what do I need a bookkeeper for? It's just an expense I don't need to take on right now." Let me ask you what you would say to one of your customers who think they can do what you do themselves so why do they need you. And the answer would be – a professional brings knowledge and experience to the problem or need which means the job gets done better, quicker and less expensively.   No matter the focus of your business you have acquired an education and the experience necessary to perform your services or provide your product while your customer has not either because of lack of time, money, or interest. So is it true with a professional bookkeeper. Yes, you or your family member/friend can help you with bill paying or invoicing but that is such a small part of the bookkeeping function.

You are the business owner and depending on your company's needs and budget you are responsible for sales, production, customer service as well as many other functions. Why not hire someone to handle the bookkeeping, a function you probably don't want to do and most certainly have no training to do. This is where outsourcing comes in. When you choose to outsource your bookkeeping functions you save time and expense. You will not incur payroll tax expenses, worker's compensation and liability insurance expenses as you would should you hire an in-house bookkeeper. Also any benefit plan costs such as vacation and sick time, and health insurance will be eliminated. The cost of setting up an office space with a desk and computer will also not be necessary. Once you have found the right person to work with, you can forget recruiting, interviewing and training costs.

Your time is needed for the building of your business and too valuable to be investing it into educating yourself to be a bookkeeper. While you need to understand the end results and how they affect your success, you can't be performing the bookkeeping functions yourself. The costs incurred to outsource your bookkeeping functions will be offset by the savings accumulated on taxes paid, tax preparation fees and more profit due to better understanding your business's financial picture.

The cost of an ongoing accurate and well maintained bookkeeping system is an expense you should build into your business budget from the beginning. The businesses that succeed made this decision early on, those who chose to delay or forgo taking their bookkeeping needs seriously either close up or have a very long and hard journey ahead.

Choosing Your Tools

When considering a bookkeeping system your first decision should be what software you will use. After choosing the accounting software then and only then choose the computer that will run your software. The reason to select your software first and computer second is that it's very important to make sure that the computer you purchase will run your new software at its peak performance levels. There is nothing more frustrating than having a software package that is slowed down or has functions that do not perform as well as they should because your computer does not have the power, memory or hard disk space you need. When you look at the requirement list that the software manufacturer recommends, always, but always, choose your computer with the highest level of software recommended requirements. Do not go by the minimum requirements. This is like buying a truck that will tow a heavy load just fine while traveling on a straight away and expecting it not to struggle when towing that load up a mountain.

With so many products to choose from where do you begin?   With you, your employees and of course your business. The very first step is to make a list (and yes, write it down) of what you expect to gain from this purchase.   Gain vs costs including costs of training and the associated costs of your time and your employees' time is a very important comparison to make. Some considerations you may want to think about are:

1. What types of information do I need the software to track?

2. What types of reports do I need, showing what data, in what format?

3. Are there particular functions my company cannot do without?

4. Who will be using the program? How many people will be using the program?

5. How comfortable are you and your employees using software and computers in general?

6. Are there programs that you are already familiar with - do you want to consider a program with a similar format?

7. How much time do I have to devote to the research, installation and training of a new program?

8. Will I need to invest in new computers, server equipment, operating systems, etc?

9. What is my budget for the program, including installation, setup, data transfer if needed, training and any new equipment?

Once you have answered these questions you have a starting point for your research. At this time you can go ahead and do the research yourself, however it could save you some time and maybe a costly mistake to bring in a professional, someone who is familiar with what software packages are available and what they can do for your business. They should also be able to offer you services such as installation, setup, perhaps data transfer if you are moving from one package to another and ongoing training and support.

By having the answers to the above questions you will be able to clearly define your needs and requirements thus saving time and money.

Whatever you do, do not take shortcuts in making such a critical business decision. The right choice will be a great investment; the wrong could be a nightmare.

My recommendation would be a QuickBooks product because QuickBooks has been around for so long, is the most purchased accounting software for business, has a wonderful reputation for providing a reliable quality product and excellent support. With QuickBooks you will also be able to choose from a wide variety of software packages from Simple Start for the simplest bookkeeping tasks, to QuickBooks Pro to add on more features and functions including multiple user capability, to QuickBooks Premier with even more features and functions and packages designed for specific industries such as construction, retail, nonprofit and manufacturing.

If you need an even more powerful solution with the availability of up to thirty users, multiple locations, and a larger database capability then QuickBooks Enterprise Solutions will fit the bill.

All of these packages can take advantage of third party software tested and approved by QuickBooks, as well as integrate with QuickBooks payroll, merchant services, and Point of Sale software.

As your company grows you can upgrade your software without having to learn a whole new way of working because each QuickBooks solution works and looks similarly to the previous one. All your data will import seamlessly into the next version.

If you have ever experienced a conversion, you know how much time and money this process can cost as well as knowing that all your data will not come across in its entire detail. Often historical information is next to impossible to bring into a new package without extensive data entry.

Choose the software that will provide your company with everything that is needed today and in the next two years. Don't settle for less now and regret it later.

Which QuickBooks Version Is Right For You?

QuickBooks comes in a variety of versions, one that is just right for your business. All versions are designed with growth in mind. Should you start with Simple Start for instance, and need to grow into QuickBooks Pro you will find the switch easy to bring your data into and even easier to learn as all QuickBooks products are similar in the basics. You will not have to relearn everything from scratch as your upgraded QuickBooks product will be very familiar in looks and basic functions. You will however have additional functionality

within each higher version. Here is a a
brief description of each product
QuickBooks offers.

Simple Start: FREE - Did I say free?

Yes, I did! If you have no more than 20
customers and want to print checks, pay
bills and track expenses, create invoices
and track sales, sales taxes and customer
payments and only need one user to
access your database this easy to learn
program is for you. Also with Simple Start
you can add a fee based subscription for
QuickBooks Payroll. Buy Simple Start for a
small fee and be able to track thousands of
customers. When you have outgrown
Simple Start your data easily converts to
QuickBooks Pro or Premier. However if

you are looking for inventory control, online banking, multi-user access or the Accountant Copy features choose QuickBooks Pro as your solution.

Online Plus: Need to be able to access your bookkeeping records anywhere you are with an internet connection? QuickBooks Online Plus is a subscription web based solution that allows multi-user access to your accounting records and payroll.   If you need to track inventory, create Purchase Orders, use forecasting or advanced reporting capabilities move up to the desktop version of Premier or Enterprise Solutions. With an additional subscription payroll features are available.

QuickBooks Pro: A desktop solution that provides full general ledger accounting modules such as Accounts Payable and Accounts Receivable as well as inventory tracking features and Payroll (with a separate subscription). This version also comes with the additional features of tracking international sales & expenses with multiple currency support and Company Snapshot, a desktop view of your company's key financial information all on one screen. If your needs encompass advanced inventory solutions, forecasting or advanced reporting capabilities you should consider Premier or Enterprise Solutions.

QuickBooks for Mac: For all you

Mac users good news. In 2009 QuickBooks released a brand new version of QuickBooks Pro with many of the bells and whistles you will find in the PC version. You can convert your PC data to the Mac version!

QuickBooks Premier: This

QuickBooks product is available in industry specific editions with reports designed with the needs of these industries in mind. The industries are Construction, Non-profits,

Manufacturing & Wholesale, Professional Services and Retail. However this product is not just for those industries as it is a great solution for all types of businesses. It also provides advanced tools for inventory and purchase orders and you will be able to easily track time, expenses, and revenues by project. Easily create a business plan and sales/expense forecasts and set billing rates by employee, customer/client, position or service. For those who have businesses that need more than five concurrent users, user permissions, greater list capacity, business solutions beyond basic accounting and advanced reporting features consider Enterprise Solutions.

QuickBooks Enterprise

Solutions: QuickBooks isn't just for small businesses anymore. Designed for the needs of mid-market companies it provides the additional features of industry specific Chart of Accounts, menus and sample files. The increased power of this database allows you to track hundreds of thousands of inventory items, customers or vendors. Have 30 concurrent users across multiple locations, and security control with detailed user permissions. With ODBC compliant applications such as Microsoft Access, Excel or Crystal Reports you can run advanced custom reports. Also included with Enterprise Solutions is the

Intuit Financial Statement Writer, a report builder that combines your QuickBooks database with the power of Microsoft Excel enabling you to build custom financial statements and reports.

Remember no matter what QuickBooks product you select as your company grows and changes you can move up to another edition that is a more robust version. Start with the edition that meets your needs now and for the next year or two and then reevaluate your QuickBooks solution as your company's needs change.

Intuit, the parent company of QuickBooks products, provides access to many other products as add-ons to meet your individual needs. Some of these are various payroll solutions, point of sales solutions including retail store hardware and online store solutions, Merchant Service solutions and even can provide you with the tools you need to select, prepare and record the necessary paperwork for the formation of your company, such as incorporation, partnership, LLC's etc through the My Corporation web site.

Intuit's Market Place also supplies a listing of third party add-on programs that integrate with QuickBooks.

All The Accounting A Business Owner Needs To Know

Even though you may not be the one who performs the tasks of keeping your books and financial records up to date, as a business owner you will need to know what reports you need to review on a regular basis and understand some key terms.

When you keep books for a company, you want to track:

Where your income comes from

What is owed you at any given time

What your expenses are and how to track to them

How you paid them

What you own at any given time

How much profit you have made (or lost)

What is your business net worth

You track this flow of money through the chart of accounts.

About the chart of accounts

The chart of accounts is a complete list of your business' accounts and their balances. Each account belongs to a segment, or group, that identifies its purpose in your financial records.   For example, your checking account would be included in your Cash accounts. Your Cash Accounts group would come under Current Assets which will be located under the general heading of Assets.

The accounts in the Chart of Accounts accumulate your financial transactions as they are posted and this information is used to produce your financial statements.

In double entry bookkeeping (the method most commonly used today) a single transaction posts to at least two accounts and sometimes more.

Each type of account listed on the Chart of Accounts has a "natural" balance type. It may be a Debit type account or a Credit type account. General Assets and Expense accounts are Debit type accounts and Liabilities, Income and Equity accounts are Credit type accounts. This means that to increase the balance of a Debit type account the entry would be to debit the account and to reduce the balance a credit entry would be made. For credit type

43

accounts the method is just the opposite - a credit entry would increase the balance and a debit entry would decrease the balance.

Assets, Liabilities, and Equity - Your Balance Sheet Accounts

Assets

Asset accounts include what you own and what people owe you. There are three general segments of Assets - Current Assets, Non-current Assets and Fixed Assets.

A Current Asset is anything you own or is owed to you that can be readily converted to cash within one year. These would include Cash, Accounts Receivables, and Inventory.

A Fixed Asset is an item you own who's worth will exceed a one year period, usually a piece of equipment, vehicle, etc. This segment will also include one or more contra-accounts called Allowance for Depreciation. A contra-account is an account which has a balance that is opposite than the normal balance type account included in the segment. An Allowance for Depreciation account normal balance is a credit type while a Fixed Asset account's balance type is Debit.

A Non-current asset is an asset that will not be converted in cash within the first year of its life. An example of this type of asset is a long-term note receivable.

Liabilities

What your company owes to other businesses, agencies or people. Liabilities are broken down into two types - Current and Non-current. Current Liabilities are amounts owed to others that are due to be paid in less than one year. They may include Accounts Payable, Payroll Tax Liabilities, Employee Benefit Liabilities, Short-term Note Payables, Customer Deposits, as well as others.

Non-Current Liabilities are amounts you owe that will be paid over a time period of more than one year. They would include Mortgages, Note Payables with longer payment terms and any other type of loans who's payment terms extend beyond one year.

Equity

Equity is the difference between what you own plus what is owed to you and what you owe. Or your company's net worth. The basic formula for a balance sheet is Equity = Assets – Liabilities or what you own less what you owe equals your net worth. Your Equity accounts include your or your partners/members initial investments, any draws or liquidations of assets (pay outs to you or partners/members in either cash or other assets), current earnings or losses and historical earnings or losses (contained in an account called Retained Earnings).

You should know, however, that net worth does not always relate to the actual market value of your company. The market value may exceed your net worth but can also be lower than your booked net worth. Market value can be affected by current values of assets being higher or lower than what is booked in your records and the assumption of goodwill your business has built as well as many other reasons. These considerations are intangibles that cannot be recorded as absolutes and therefore are not part of your financial records.

Your equity balance can be changed by an increase or reduction of other balance sheet account balances and reported profit or loss. For example if your assets increase your equity will show an improved balance. The same for a reduction in liabilities or an increase of profits. However should your assets decrease (less cash in the bank is a common reason for this) or your liabilities increase or you are reporting a loss than your equity balance will suffer. Of course these events might occur in combination, and your equity accounts will be affected by the net change.

Cash versus accrual bookkeeping

There are two types of accounting methods a business owner needs to choose between.

Cash basis

Income is recorded when money from sales is received and expenses when bills are paid.

Accrual basis

Income is recorded at the time of the sale regardless of payment terms and expenses are recorded when you receive the bill whether or not they have been paid for.

QuickBooks allows you to view your financial statements on both a Cash and an Accrual Basis, however if you are using Accounts Receivable and Accounts Payable accounts your Cash Basis reports will not automatically show the correct amounts. There is a work around for these issues, but it would be easier for you to choose one or the other method from the start. If you will be booking your sales with invoices and expect them to be paid at a later date then you will be using the Accounts Receivable features. If you will be booking your expenses ahead of paying them then you will be using the Accounts Payable feature. Using the

Accounts Receivable and Accounts Payable accounts means you are choosing an Accrual Basis. To choose to use either one or both of these accounts and report on a cash basis means you will be using a hybrid of both methods which will require adjustments for reporting and tax purposes.

Unless you are strictly a cash business - you get paid at the time of service or sale of product and you pay your vendors when you receive their services or product, I would recommend you choose the Accrual Basis. Check with your tax preparer and/or accountant before making this decision.

Should you decide that the Cash Basis is the better solution for you then use the Sales Receipt function instead of Create Invoices and post the checks you write into your check register instead of using the Enter Bills feature. These two methods will post your sales and expenditures directly to your cash accounts instead of posting transactions to either Accounts Receivable or Accounts Payable.

Basic Financial Reports

The Balance sheet

A snapshot of your company as of a particular date. It shows:

What you own and what is owed to you. (assets)

What your business owes (liabilities)

The net worth of your business   (equity)

The Profit and Loss Statement (Income Statement)

A profit and loss statement or income statement shows income, expenses, and net profit or loss for a specific period of time.

Statement of Cash Flows

Shows receipts and payments and the effect on available cash during a specific accounting period or what cash came in and from where it came and what cash went out and where it went to.

Accounts Receivable Aging

A list of which customers have unpaid invoices, how much they owe and whether they are current or over due. With a summary report the list is a total per customer while a detailed report will show each unpaid invoice.

Accounts Payable Aging

A list of vendors you owe, how much you owe each vendor and whether you are current or overdue with your payments.

As with the Accounts Receivable Aging you can choose between a summary report (total owed per vendor) or a detailed report (lists each unpaid invoice for each vendor).

There are, of course many other reports you may wish to consider viewing, but these are the ones you want to make sure you review on a monthly basis.

So many new and existing business owners do not review this data until the end of their year when taxes are due to be prepared or sometimes not even then. They just give the data file to their tax preparer and hope for the best.

If you pay attention to these reports each and every month you won't have any unpleasant surprises at the end of the year. Even more importantly, monthly reviews will enable you to see trends in your business when you can step in and make a difference.

Decisions can be made to invest in new equipment, employees, or marketing if your reports point to positive growth. Perhaps you are spending too much money in areas that you should be cutting back. You won't know that if you don't know where you are spending your money, what your sales growth is or if you are making a profit.

You could be leaving money on the table by letting your clients go too long in paying you. Vendors discounts could be missed or late charges accumulated by not knowing when your bills are due.

Setting Up Your Books

Now that you have decided on your system and understand a few common terms that every business owner or bookkeeper needs to know to get the most out of their bookkeeping system, it is time to discover what has to be done to have clear, concise, and correct financial records.

You have chosen your accounting package, decided you are going to take your bookkeeping tasks seriously, and are ready to get started.

Both your bookkeeper and you, the business owner, should know what steps need to be taken to correctly set up your bookkeeping system. Even if as owner you are not directly performing the bookkeeping tasks for your business it is important for you to be aware of how your system is setup so you can ascertain that the process is being done correctly. After all, it is your business and so the record keeping may be delegated but the prime responsibility is yours for accurate records. Also there may be certain information you might ✳ want to enter yourself to protect your privacy.

QuickBooks walks you through a Setup
Wizard with clear and easy steps to get
you started. When you first start
QuickBooks you will be taken to a "Get
Started" screen. If this screen does not
appear you can also reach this screen
by selecting the File menu and selecting
the menu item titled "New Company".

Clicking on the button labeled "Start
Interview" will start the wizard. Before
starting this interview, refer to Appendix
D at the end of this book for a handy list
of the information you should gather
first.

The first order of business is to enter your company's information. Name, address, phone numbers, e-mail address, web site and Tax ID number. The Company Name field is required and shows a red asterisk as an indicator. The others can be filled in later if you don't have the information readily available at this time. However you will want to make sure to obtain this information and add it to your database ASAP. You can add this information later by accessing the Company menu and selecting Company Information.

The next screen asks you to identify your type of business. This selection helps QuickBooks to define a prebuilt Chart of Accounts. Choose a business type that is the closest to your company. If no selection is right for your business, don't worry, just select either the General Product-based or General Service-based Business depending on whether your company sells products or provides services. If you sell products and provide services choose the type that is your predominate income source.

QuickBooks also uses this selection to automatically enable features that are commonly needed in a particular type of business. For example if you are a retail store than QuickBooks will enable sales tax features. If you are in some type of construction QuickBooks will add the Estimate feature. However, no matter which type you choose you will be able to make changes to the Chart of Accounts and to the features that will reside in your database.

QuickBooks now asks what type of entity your company is, such as Sole Proprietorship, Partnership, Corporation, etc. If you are not sure which to use, it is best to ask your accountant or tax preparer. You can also determine this by the tax form you have been filing for this company if you have been in business for at least one tax year. After each entity type you will see the tax form number listed. Check last year's tax form for the number. If you are a sole proprietorship your tax return will be your personal tax return which is Form 1040. If you have changed your entity type - during the current year - perhaps you were a sole proprietor last year but took on a partner or decided to incorporate this year than choose the current type of entity for your company.

Select the first month of your fiscal year. A fiscal year is defined as a twelve month financial period used to accumulate your financial transactions for reporting and tax purposes.   Once you have selected a fiscal year for your company you should not change it without knowing the effect the change will have on your reporting and tax requirements.

For most small businesses this will be January (even if you are starting your company or database in another month) which is referred as the calendar year - January through December. However some companies may have a non-calendar fiscal year. In this case the month you select will be the first month of your fiscal year. This is a decision you should discuss with your accountant if you are starting a new company. If you have been in business awhile then your past year's tax return will tell you what your tax preparer has been using.

Set up your Administrator's user password. Don't skip this step as it is a very important key to good security. There is an audit report function in QuickBooks that allows you to determine who has made or changed transactions by user. If you don't set up a password and all users are allowed to use the Administrator's log in than there is no way to determine who has made or changed transactions.

Keep your password close to your chest. Accountants and/or outsourced bookkeepers can be added to the user list with all the functions they need and can have unique log-in names and passwords.

There can be only one Administrator per database. If your bookkeeper is setting up the database, you can enter the Admin password later. Although this is one reason why you should be going through this wizard yourself.

Now QuickBooks is ready to create your company file. Click Next.

Save your file in your My Documents folder in a new folder named QuickBooks Data Files. You of course can name the folder whatever makes sense to you.

The reason to do this is to locate the file in a place that it can remain in and can also be easily found. Once you have saved the file QuickBooks will automatically navigate to this folder and open the file when you start up QuickBooks.

If you are setting up more than one database for different companies, you should set up a separate folder in the QuickBooks Data Files folder for each company.

This is also the place you will want to save backup, portable or Accountant's Copy files when they are created. If you move the file once you have saved it (which often happens when a file is saved to a desktop) QuickBooks will not be able to locate it when you open the program and you will have to locate it yourself. Another reason to have clearly marked folders designated.

The file name will be the name of your company followed by a .qbw extension. The different types of QuickBooks files end in different extensions which can be found in Appendix B. You may change the file name at this point should you wish, it will not change the company name in the database, however.

As you work in QuickBooks and create backups, portable files, and Accountant's Copy files you might want to add a date or some other identification to the file name in able to identify the file to restore if necessary.

QuickBooks creates the company database.

You are now ready to customize your database. QuickBooks asks "what do you sell?" Select one of three choices that reflects your company.

Do you charge sales tax? You should know your state's regulations or ask your accountant to help with this question. As in other areas you can change your mind about this later but it should be answered before you start posting transactions. Depending upon the type of business you selected previously QuickBooks will make a recommendation for your business.

Do you want to create estimates? Again this option can be added or deleted later and QuickBooks will make a recommendation.

Do you want to use Sales Receipts? Invoices are for billings to customer that will be paid in the future, Sales Receipts are for payments at the time of purchase or services rendered. If you have chosen a Cash Basis, select yes. If you have chosen an Accrual Basis you can use both Sales Receipts and Invoices depending on the way and time you are getting paid.

Using Statements? Choose Yes or No depending upon whether you provide monthly statements to your clients which list outstanding charges and invoices. As well as late payment fees, interest charges, etc.

Using Invoices? If you are not receiving full payment at the time of selling a product or providing a service you can use the Invoice function to record the sale and the amount owed into Accounts Receivable. Use the Accrual Basis if you choose to use Invoices.

Progress Invoices are used when you are billing a client through out the project you have contracted with them. A good example of this is a contractor who prepares a contract for work to be done over a period of time and the work is to be paid at agreed upon intervals as the work is completed. You would bill using the Progress Invoice feature. Choose yes if you will be billing in this way or no if you only bill when you have provided the service or product in its entirety.

Managing Bills You Owe? If you want to track bills prior to paying them then say yes to this option. An Accounts Payable account will be set up and you will use the Enter Bills and Pay Bills features to enter your bills and pay them.

If you are going to enter your bill payments directly in your checkbook register or use the Write Checks feature then answer no to this question. If you are using Accounts Payable transactions then you should select Accrual Basis and if you are posting bill payments directly into your checkbooks register you should choose the Cash Basis.

Do You Print Checks? Will you or do you want to print your checks directly out of QuickBooks? If so select the "I Print Checks" answer. Not sure then check the next answer, QuickBooks will remind you that you have this option available and give you the resources to order the checks and deposits slips you need.   Of course if you are either hand writing checks or doing electronic payments directly from your bank then the third answer is the one to choose.

Do you now or would you like to in the future accept credit card payments from your clients? Choose the appropriate answer for this question depending on your current or future needs. This decision can be revisited at a later time.

Tracking Time in QuickBooks - QuickBooks has a time tracking feature that allows you to enter yours, or employee's time and subcontractor's time to be billed and have the time charged to a client. The employee's rate and the charge out rate can be different. Choose either yes or no. This option can be turned on or off later should you wish.

Do You Have Employees? W-2 employees are people that you hire, give payroll checks to and deduct and remit payroll taxes for.

1099 employee's are subcontractors. There are government definitions of what an employee vs a subcontractor is and this designation is dependent on how the subcontractor works with your company. In Appendix C there is a discussion regarding the difference between an employee and a subcontractor. If you have neither at this time then select NO.

Tracking Multiple Currencies - If you are selling outside of the USA you may want to select this option. It allows you to bill and receive payments with automatic adjustments for foreign currency exchange differences. This is one area where a choice cannot be turned off once you have selected to turn it on. If you are not sure, select NO as you can turn it on later should you need this option. This feature first became available in 2009.

Choosing a start date - before going on you need to decide when your books will start. If you are at the beginning of your fiscal year the decision is easy, the date you will use is the first day of the current year. For example if you are using a calendar fiscal year, the start date you will use will be January 1st of the current year. However if you are further into the year you might want to start with balances from the end of the last quarter, or the last month, etc. Use the first day of the quarter or month in which you want to start. It all depends on how much transaction details you want to post into the new database.

Add Your Bank Account - You should have the last reconciled bank statement available that corresponds with the starting date you have chosen. For example, if you have chosen a starting date of January 1st, you should have available December 31st reconciled bank statement.

Enter your bank account information as needed making sure that the required fields are completed. The bank account name and routing number can be filled in later if you don't have the information available at this time. Choose when the bank account was started. This is dependent on the starting date you chose earlier.

Fill in the bank statement information asked on the next screen. If you have checks dated in the period before your start date that did not clear on the last bank statement then subtract them from the bank statement balance. Also if deposits did not clear that were dated in the period before your start date then add them to the bank statement balance.

You will make an entry in the check register using the prior period ending date for the uncleared checks and deposits. This is so you can reconcile these checks and deposits for the end of the first accounting period in QuickBooks. They will be entered with the last date of the prior period once the Interview process is completed.

QuickBooks now asks if you would like to add additional bank accounts. You can either enter them now or later, but you should enter a separate bank account for each account you have even if they are at the same bank. Bank accounts include checking, money market accounts, saving accounts, etc.

Now you have the opportunity to review and add or delete accounts from the Chart of Accounts. Check the accounts you would like to use and uncheck the accounts you would like not to use.

Accounts can be added, renamed, made inactive or deleted at a later time. The only restriction is that you cannot delete an account once you have posted transactions to it, but you can make it inactive which means you won't see it in your list of accounts anymore, but it will show up on your reports should there be a balance. These are the accounts QuickBooks is recommending based on the type of business you chose earlier in the interview.

You have now completed the Set Up Interview! Click on Finish.

A QuickBooks Coach window will popup offering you tutorials, training options, or you can just dive right in.

Setting Up Users

Should you have more than one person with access to your books you will want your first task to be the setting up of users and granting the appropriate permissions to those users.

By default, QuickBooks assigns the User "Admin" when the database is first created. This is usually the business owner's user account and should have a secure password. There can only be one Administrator in a QuickBooks database. The administrator has access to all functions in the database, but only the administrator can do the following:

Add a user and assign permissions

Change a user's access permissions

Import and export data

Apply for QuickBooks merchant services

Change company information such as company name, address, or fiscal year

Change Company wide preferences

Set a Closing Date and Closing Password

Do not allow all users to use the Admin log-on user name and password because the Administrator has access to all QuickBooks functions and all levels of information.

Users should only have access to those functions that allow them to do their job. For example, a person handling Accounts Receivable functions does not need access to vendor and vendor related tasks, payroll or non Accounts Receivable reports.

If you have more than one person working in your QuickBooks data file, it is always a good idea to have each user handle a specialized area of your bookkeeping functions with only one (the Administrator) having access to all functions.

If each user has a unique log-in then it is easier to determine who and when transactions were posted, changed, or voided by reviewing the Audit Report (Report menu/Accountant & Taxes/ Audit Report).

To set up a new user (only the
administrator can perform this task)
select the Company pull down menu
and then choose Set Up Users and
Passwords. You then choose between
Set Up Users, Change Your Password,
or Buy Additional User License. Select
Set Up Users.

In the window that opens you will see a
list of the users already active. At this
screen you may add a new user, edit an
existing user, delete a user, and view a
user. You can also set a closing date
for your books in this screen. Select
Add User. Assign a user name and
password.

Passwords should be considered carefully. While most people choose to pick a password that is easily remembered this is not the most secure way to protect your all important financial data.

Names of pets, birthdays or anniversaries, favorite things or hobbies, kids names, etc are the first guesses for anyone trying to access your information.

Therefore, passwords should contain six or more characters and these characters should be a combination of both letters and numbers.

Arbitrary non-word and non-specific to the user are the best passwords. Harder to remember, but also almost impossible for anyone to guess. While discussing passwords, the administrator's password should be the most complicated of all.

Keep a record of all password's assigned (only the business owner and/ or the person assigned the Administrator user functions) should have access to all the passwords.

Do not allow your users to write down the password to be kept in their desks, or paperwork, diaries, etc. They should memorize their password and if then they forget (which if they are using the password on a daily basis should not be a problem) they can either ask the person that holds the list or the administrator can assign them a new password.

All passwords should be changed every 90 days from it issuance. Any time an employee leaves the company or their job function changes the user account should be deleted immediately.

With today's technology allowing people to log in to computers remotely you cannot be too careful in protecting your data.

You can add this new user to your QuickBook's license in this screen by clicking on the button provided. I am now going to discuss the different types of permissions that can be given users and this information is related to the QuickBooks Pro, Premier and Accountant editions. Enterprise Solutions has the ability to be more specific in the permissions that users can be assigned. And will not be covered in this discussion.

Click Next.

The next screen asks you whether you want this user to have selected areas of QuickBooks or all areas of QuickBooks. Most likely you will be choosing to have the user to have selected areas.   Click Next to begin assigning the user's permissions.

QuickBooks will now present you with several screens where you can assign No Access, Full Access or Selective access to each of the functional areas in QuickBooks. Those areas are:

Sales and Accounts Receivable

Purchases and Accounts Payable

Checking and Credit Cards

Inventory

Time Tracking

Payroll and Employees

Sensitive Accounting Activities

Sensitive Financial Reporting

Changing or Deleting Transactions

Each of the areas presented describe what functions a user will have and what reports they will have access to.

The No Access choice means that this user will not be able to use or view any of the functions listed in the description provided.

Full access means they will be able to access, post, and view reports for all the functions listed in the description. Selective Access allows you to decide that the user will only be able to Create Transactions, Create and Print Transactions, or Create Transactions, and Create Reports.

Make your choices carefully and only give permissions that are needed for this particular user to do their job.

Two of the area screens have unique areas to consider. They are as follows:

Sales and Accounts Receivable - there is a box asking whether you want this user to have access to customer complete credit card numbers. You should review your merchant services PCI DSS requirements to make sure you are abiding by the standards set for protection of your customers' credit card payment data. Not complying with these standards can lead to a security breach and significant fines for you and your company. So check this box with care and with full knowledge of the risks that may be involved.

Changing or Deleting Transactions -
the questions asked on this screen are
whether you want the user to be able to
make changes or to delete transactions
within the area(s) they have been given
permission to access and whether you
want them to be able to change or
delete transactions that were dated
before the closing date set in your
database.

These answers will depend on your trust in your employees accessing the database not only in their honesty but also in their knowledge of how these changes or deletions will affect your books, both now and in the past. I would strongly suggest that these functions are available to only the business owner, or head of the accounting/bookkeeping department.

Once you have made your selections you will be presented with a list of the permissions and the permission levels that you have assigned this user. You can use the Back button to change the selections you have made. Of course you can always edit the permissions of the user at a later time if necessary.

Click Finish to save this user.

You may also want to set up a specific user for your CPA, or tax preparer if they will have access to your database.

By having a unique user name for every person accessing your QuickBooks database you can track who did what and when. Very important when tracking down posting errors, changes and deletions made and determining whether some hanky-panky is going on by a less then honest employee or consultant. Better safe than sorry!

Setting Up Preferences

QuickBooks can be customized to your needs by reviewing the Preferences which can be found by selecting the Edit menu and selecting the Preferences menu option.

There are two types of Preferences - "My Preferences" and "Company Preferences". Company Preferences are those that will affect all users while My Preferences are those that are set for the individual user. Only the Administrator can change the Company Preferences. A User with the appropriate security can change My Preferences and these preferences are mostly about the way you navigate within the database and how the database looks.

On the left hand side of the screen you will see an alphabetic list of the different types of preferences. Clicking on a preference type in this section will change the window to show you the preferences that are available for that type. Not all preference types will have both My Preferences and Company Preferences.

If you remember, in the setup wizard you made some decisions on how QuickBooks would run for your company. You were also told that these choices could be changed in some cases. This is the area where you can make those changes.

Below is a list of some of the preferences you should definitely pay attention to.

Accounting Preferences: Under the Company Preferences tab you can choose to use Account numbers and to require all accounts. If you use a numbering system (see Appendix E for suggested numbering schemes) your Chart of Accounts can be organized more easily. QuickBooks by default orders your Chart of Accounts alphabetically within an account type. Which means you might find your accounts listed in a way that doesn't make sense.

By using numbers your accounts will fall into their place because you choose the position by assigning the number. This will keep you from moving accounts around every time you set up a new account. Having your accounts in the order that they belong in will make your financial statements look more professional and easier to read.

Checking off the box Require Accounts ascertains that an account will be assigned to every transaction when it is posted. Should you forget, you will receive a warning.

Show Lowest Subaccount Only keeps users from posting to a parent account instead of the subaccount. If the parent account does not show up in the list to choose from, then they cannot accidentally choose the wrong account to post to. Find more information about parent and subaccounts in Appendix E.

Class Tracking is the way QuickBooks handles breaking out income and expenses into departments, locations, geographical areas, etc.

You should note that you can only choose one type of class. This means that you can have QuickBooks track by location, but not departments. Or by sales reps, but not by store. We will discuss setting up the classes later, for now all you need to do is to decide whether you want to use classes and if so if you want to be given a warning if you have forgotten to add the class to the transaction.

The Date Warnings are useful to make sure you are not posting transactions in a prior or future year, quarter or month. You get to choose how many days in the past or future.

While posting transactions it can be easy to key in a wrong date in the date field. QuickBooks will warn you should you type in a date that is either beyond or prior to the days you select in this preference.

The Closing Date Preference is one you should choose. The idea is to prevent any user from posting in a prior year thus changing the closed fiscal year. You will set a date which should be the end of the prior year.

One caveat, if you are working near to the end of the year and are still making adjusting entries you might want this date to allow postings in the last month of the year. In any case you will be able to make those entries even though the closing date has gone past. You will need a password to perform this task. The password should be different from anyone's log in password (including the administrator') and should only be given to the person who has the knowledge and the authority to make these types of entries.

Billing Preferences: This is where you can set your default payment terms for vendors, decide whether you would like to receive a warning that you have entered a duplicate vendor invoice number, and requests that discounts and credits be applied immediately to the earliest dated unpaid invoice when payments are being issued. You can also define a discount account to be used.

Checking Preferences: On the My Preferences tab you can assign default accounts to be used for Write Checks, Pay Bills, Pay Sales Tax and Make Deposits.

Should you have more than one bank account you might want to assign accounts for these functions here. Of course, you can change the account to use when posting the transaction if necessary.

On the Company Preference tab you will see that you have options on what appears on your checks, and whether to have QuickBooks give you a warning if a duplicate check number is used.

There is also a section to define default accounts for payroll and payroll tax payments. You can choose how your On-line Banking information is presented. Side-by-side mode offers you a form type listing of the transactions to be matched or added and renaming rules are more flexible. In the Register mode you can use the account register to add or match transactions. You can change this at any time by returning to this preference screen.

Desktop View: This is where you can select the icons you would like to appear on your Home page. In the Company Preference tab under Related Preferences you can turn on or off several different types of functions.

When you click on one of these items you will be taken to the preference type it refers to. For example should you click on the Sales Tax listing to turn it on, note that the Sales Tax preference type in the left hand section automatically hi lights the Sales Tax preference type.

Your preference window will also reflect the options available for the one you choose, in the example you will see a window that lists all the sales tax options.

Turning off the features you don't need will eliminate the associated icon from your Home page. This is an easy way to simplify your Home page.

On the My Preferences tab you can select several ways to see what will appear when QuickBooks opens including a color scheme. Remember the option changes on this tab are set by the one user making the changes and will not affect what other users see.

Finance Charges: Set default interest and late payment charges to be issued to your clients and how and when they will be charged.

General Preferences: The My Preferences here are choices on how to navigate within the program. Company Preferences give you the option to choose how time and dates are presented, whether to save transactions before printing and whether to update name information when saving transactions.

Integrated Applications: This is where you can add third party software to QuickBooks and give permission for the software to access your database.

Items and Inventory: If you are not tracking inventory you can skip this section. However if you are interested in tracking inventory than this is where you would make the inventory and purchase order functions active.

You can choose to be warned if duplicate purchase order numbers are entered and decide how you want to be alerted to low inventory levels for individual products.

If you are using QuickBooks Premier or Enterprise Solutions you can set up the Unit of Measure feature here.

The Unit of Measure feature allows you to buy in one type of unit and then sell in another. For example a store buying and selling can goods might buy in cases but sell individual cans. This feature allows you to track inventory easily without setting up two different inventory items.

Jobs and Estimates: If you are interested in producing estimates for your clients and/or tracking job costing this is where you can choose to have these functions available in QuickBooks.

Progress Invoicing allows you to bill and track the billing in increment amounts against an estimate as the job continues.

Multiple Currencies: Do you have customers or vendors that are out of the United States and would you like to make payments and collect receivables using multiple currencies? If so, QuickBooks makes it easy for you by taking care of all the behind the scene exchange rate transactions. Select this feature and choose the currency you are using for your business. For most of you this will be US Currency. Since QuickBooks is available in other countries you might want to choose another currency. This feature first became available in 2009.

Payments: QuickBooks offers a variety of ways for you to get paid besides checks or cash. This screen is where you can get started with receiving your payments through Intuits different Payment Solutions. These solutions do require an application process and are fee based. You can find more information about these services by clicking on the Get Started links. This screen also offers options on how to handle receipts when they are posted into QuickBooks. The default for Use Undeposited Funds as a default deposit to account is checked. I suggest you leave the default.

When you go to the bank to make a deposit you might have several checks from various customers to deposit at the same time. Those checks might have been received over a period of time but the bank will record the entire deposit with the date that you bring them to the bank. This is how they will show up on your bank statement.

If you record each deposit as it is received with the date of receipt and post them directly to the checking account you will have a hard time matching up the individual entries to the one deposit listed on your bank statement.

QuickBooks has a solution for this. By posting all deposits to the Undeposited Funds account you can use the Deposit Funds function to choose the individual entries that make up a specific deposit. QuickBooks will then remove the individual entries from the Undeposited Fund account and post the combined receipts into one deposit into the check register. When you reconcile your bank account, only the entry made in your check register will show making it easy for you to reconcile.

Payroll: Will you be using one of QuickBooks solutions? Choose Full Payroll if you are or will be using QuickBooks Basic, Standard, Enhanced or Assisted Payroll. If you plan on manually calculating payroll yourself.

If you have no employees or are using an outside payroll service select the No Payroll option. If you are or will be using Intuit Payroll Services Complete Payroll select that option.

If you choose either the No Payroll or Complete Payroll option the only preferences you will have available is how your employees names are listed in the Employee List.

If you choose Full Payroll then other options are ready to be selected and set up. Clicking on the Pay Stub & Voucher Printing will open a screen where you can choose what will show up on these documents.

Clicking on the Worker's Compensation button opens a screen to add the functions of tracking worker's compensation, opt to receive a warning if a code is not selected, and to exclude the overtime paid in the worker's compensation calculation. You should check with your insurance agent or accountant to determine how your state handles overtime regarding worker's compensation.

The Sick and Vacation button opens a window where you can set up how QuickBooks handles these benefits. This is a company wide default. In Payroll you can override this default if needed.

The Employee Default option allows you to set up an employee default that can be used to automatically set up a new employee. When adding an employee you can choose to use the default employee configuration and then make changes to those items that are unique to the new employee.

Before you use this section you should be familiar with payroll, employee records, payroll items and payroll tax items.

Reminders: Check off what reminders you want QuickBooks to alert you to and when you want to see the alert.

Reports & Graphs: My Preferences presents option on how reports and graphs are displayed and refresh options.

On the Company Preferences tab you can choose whether the reports are presented using an accrual or cash basis, how the aging reports are calculated, how the accounts are displayed, and lets you customize your Cash Flow Reports organization.

Sales & Customers: In My Preferences you can select how time and costs are added to invoices when job costing, and adding a payment tool bar on Receive Payment and Sales Receipt forms.

On the Company Preference tab you can select a default shipping method, choose a default template for packing slips, opt to use pricing levels, and enable Sales Orders.

Pricing levels allow you to set a single price for an item or service you sell and then assign a level for individual customers automating customized priced invoices.   The levels can be based on fixed percentage or per item levels if you are using QuickBooks Premier or Enterprise Solutions.

Sales orders allow you to process a single invoice for multiple orders, partial invoicing, or backorder tracking.

Sales Tax: You will need to gather some information and perhaps ask your accountant for some help to complete this preference set up. However the first decision is whether you need to collect sales tax. If not, just select the NO option and go on to the next preference.

If yes, you need to know the laws in your state regarding the collection and paying of sales tax. You also should be aware of the laws governing your sales tax requirements for other states should you sell products/services beyond your state lines or on the internet. Once you are armed with this information you can return to this screen to fill out the information needed. I strongly suggest if you are responsible to collect and pay sales tax for the products or services you sell you do not add any invoices until this screen is filled out correctly.

Send Forms: On the My Preferences tab select what email program you are using and select whether you would like to default a customer's preferred send method to "is to be e-mailed". QuickBooks uses either Microsoft Outlook (not Outlook Express, however) or QuickBooks email. With QuickBooks email your email is sent through Intuit's secure email server.

On the Company Preference tab you can write a default e-mail note for several types of documents being sent. These are invoices, estimates, statements, sales orders, sales receipts, credit memos, purchase orders, reports and paystubs. Each type of document can have a separate default message.

Service Connection: When QuickBooks is installed these preferences are automatically set up. Unless you have a specific reason for changing these preferences I would not change the defaults.

Spelling: Can you imagine sending out a client document with one or more spelling errors? How embarrassing! QuickBooks solves this problem with a built-in spell checker. Check off the Always check spelling box and never have this problem again. You can also customize the spell checker by telling QuickBooks to ignore certain common phases as listed on this screen.

TAX: 1099 The IRS mandates that companies that make certain types of payments to vendors report those payments at the end of the year using a 1099 form.

The 1099 MISC form has several blocks for summarizing different types of payments you may have made during the year. This window lists those blocks and allows you to choose accounts with transactions that include those specific type of payments.

Make sure if you are choosing a Rent account, for example, to assign to the 1099 Rent category it only includes Rent payments that are required by law to be reported on this form.

The IRS also assigns thresholds for each 1099 category type. You are not required to file the 1099 if a vendor has not met the threshold.

You should speak to your accountant to determine which categories you need to assign accounts to, how those accounts should be set up and what the individual thresholds are.

If you are required to report interest payments you will have to prepare the 1099 INT form either manually or use a separate form software package. QuickBooks only supports the 1099 MISC form at this time.

Time and Expenses: Under the Company Preference tab you can choose to track time and expenses.

If you choose to track time and expenses then you have the option to have these entries as a list of items to be billed appear when you are preparing a client invoice.

You can also set a default markup percentage and an account to record the markup to.

Also you can choose to have your reimbursable expenses posted to an income account.   Choose this option if you want the reimbursement kept separate from the expense you paid. If you are charging sales tax on the reimbursable expense this is the preferred way to use.

Setting Up Items:

So just what are Items and do I need or want to use them? The first answer is that an Item is a QuickBooks feature that helps you automate the filling out of various forms such as invoices, sales receipts, purchase orders, bills, and estimates.

Once set up correctly selecting an item from the pull down list, a description, cost or price and other information you would like to show up in the form you are creating is automatically filled in saving you time and assuring that you are consistent in the information you are presenting to clients and vendors.

Items also take care of accurately posting the entries being made behind the scene. For each item you can assign a sales account and if needed a cost of goods sold or expense account. When you save a form that posts to the general ledger QuickBooks posts to the accounts you have assigned to each individual item.

To set up items select the List menu and then choose Item List. Depending on the answers you gave in the Setup Wizard or the choices you made in Preferences you might already see an Item or two already listed.

You should review any item that QuickBooks created for you to determine that it is described and set up correctly.

Navigating the Item List Screen:

First lets discuss the Item List screen and the options available for you there. You can search on all the selected columns to find the item you are looking for, handy once many items are listed in your database.

In the bottom left hand corner of the screen are several menus. The first one is titled Item and has the commands to Add, Edit, Duplicate, Delete or Add Multiple Items.

Clicking on the Add Multiple Items opens a new screen which can be used to either type in multiple items with their individual information or to copy and paste the item information from a Microsoft Excel spreadsheet.

You can only add one type of Item at a time and only Service, Inventory Parts and Non-Inventory Items are available as types to be added from this screen.

You can also add Customer and Vendor information in the same way from this screen.

This screen can also be accessed through the Customer Center and Vendor Center. Click on the New Customer and Job or New Vendor button and select Add Multiple in either of these centers. You can add additional fields to this listing by clicking on the Customize button in the upper right hand corner.

Once you have filled out the list, click on Save and the data will update your Item list.

Also on the Items menu you will find options to make an Item inactive (it will remain in the database but will not show up in the pull down menus or in the Item Listing).

Because you cannot delete an Item that has postings even if the balance has gone to zero, this is an easy way to clean up your list. Also available are options to re-sort the list, print the list, customize the list columns and search for transactions.

The next menu is titled Activities and depending on the functions you have chosen QuickBooks lists several tasks that can be performed using Items such as Create Invoices and Sales Receipts, Change Prices, Build Assemblies, Create Purchase Orders, Receive Inventory and Enter Bills, Adjust Inventory Quantities and Values and Check Current Availability.

Under Reports you will find several reports including a QuickReport for any item you have hi-lighted.

The Excel menu lists the functions of exporting to Excel, pasting from Excel and Exporting All Items.

The Attach menu takes you on line to the Document Management Feature provided by QuickBooks. This online document storage and sharing feature is free for the first 100 MB which represents approximately 1000 2-page PDF documents.

If you need more space it is available for a small monthly fee. Scan your bills, statements, checks, etc and have them available digitally any time and you can put your old file cabinet in a yard sale. Because you can make this available to your tax preparer/accountant there will be no more boxes, bags and envelopes being carted to their office at tax time.

Choosing Your Item Type:

There are several types of items, some of which you may use and others which you might choose not to use.

In some types of items you will see a checkbox that reads "this service is used in assemblies, or is performed by a subcontractor or partner". Check this box if you want both the sales price to be posted to an income account and the cost of the sales to be posted to an expense account.

The Inventory Parts and Inventory Assemblies do not have this checkbox available as they already have both Purchase and Sales fields available.

Service, Non-Inventory, and Other Charge types let you choose whether you wish transactions to be posted automatically with both cost and sales amounts to accounts you designate.

However, the only time this box should not be checked is if you only want the transaction to be posted to either a general ledger sales account, **or** a cost of goods sold account/ expense account, not both.

For example if you are setting up an item to record office supplies purchases you would only want to post to an expense account because you will not be posting a sale at the same time and therefore would not check the box for this Non-Inventory type item.

If you have a question as to whether you should be using this function with a particular item then please confer with a QuickBooks Consultant, your bookkeeper or accountant.

Once checked the window will expand adding fields for the purchase information. What happens when this box is checked and both the purchase and sales information is filled in, is when saving a sales form an entry will be made to both the income account and the expense account with the appropriate dollars for each part of the transaction.

For example, should you set up a Service item with a purchase cost of $1.00 and a sales price of $2.00 the following entry will be made automatically:

	Debit	**Credit**
Cost of Goods Sold	$1.00	
Income Account		$2.00
Inventory Asset		$1.00
(reducing inventory)		
Accounts Receivable	$2.00	
(or Cash Received)		

If the box is not checked the entry made will be:

	Debit	Credit
AR or Cash	$2.00	
Account Chosen		$2.00

in the Account field when you

set up the item

In the first scenario you will post a sale to an income account, remove the appropriate cost from your inventory account and post that amount to your cost of goods account while recording the amount owed to you for this sale in Accounts Receivable.

In the second scenario, you will post the sales amount to either a sales account or cost of goods sold/expense account depending on the account chosen when the item was set up and post the amount owed to you for this sale in AR.

This would be an incorrect way of posting a sale because either your sale would not be reflected in your income account or the expense of the sale would not be recorded in your expense or cost of goods sold account. Also your used inventory would not be reflected in a reduction of your inventory account balance.

165

NOTE: If you are not tracking inventory and posting the costs of your products or services directly when you are billed by your vendors you do not need to check this box. Fill in the sale price and the income account to use when preparing an invoice to your customers. If you want to have items set up for expenses to be posted when creating either vendor bills or payments to vendors then set up a separate item to be used for purchasing the product/service and use the Rate and Accounts fields for instructions for amounts that will be posted to your expense account (can be changed at the form level).

Service Item: Even if you do not track inventory, this item should be set up for any business that provides services to a client/customer. Use for professional services, fees of any type and labor charges charged.

Inventory Part: Use this item type to track the purchase and sales of items you purchase for resale. Make sure to assign the proper accounts for both income and expense accounts.

Inventory Assemblies: Some companies buy inventory parts and then combine them to make another item which they then sell. This item can be used to automate this process.

As you add individual parts to assemble this item the cost will be calculated. Type in the total cost QuickBooks displays in the cost field.

If you have set a default markup in Preferences/Time and Billing the sales price will be filled in automatically using the default markup. You may change the sales price if necessary or add one if it is not filled in for you. Make sure to assign the proper accounts for both income and expense accounts.

When you add assemblies the inventory parts needed to build the assemblies will be removed from the individual parts items and the cost will be adjusted by any adjustments made to the costs of the individual parts.

Non-Inventory Parts: Use this item type for those items you purchase but do not track. This may be office supplies, miscellaneous parts or materials you have purchased specifically for one customer or job that you will be billing out. When setting up a Non-Inventory Part for items that you will be billing out, make sure you check the box "this service is used in assemblies, or is performed by a subcontractor or partner" and fill in both the Purchase and Sales fields with the appropriate information.

Other Charge: You might use this for delivery charges, miscellaneous labor or parts, set up fees and service fees.

Subtotal: Should you want to add a subtotal on a form this is the item type you would select. This item will subtotal all preceding lines. Should you use this and then add more items and add an additional subtotal item the second subtotal will not include the first subtotal. This can be used to apply discounts or surcharges to a list of items.

Group: You may want to break out individual items for your records when creating a sales form but only want to have your customer see a one line description and price. This is the item you would use to accomplish this task.

Add the items you want to be included in the group. This is different from an Inventory Assembly in that the tracking of cost and availability in a Group item is calculated within each individual item where with an Inventory Assembly item the cost and availability of the assembly is calculated separately because the individual items have already been relieved of the quantity and value amounts used to build the assembly.

Discount: You can set up discounts using either percentage or fixed amounts to adjust your customers billings. This is used after a subtotal or total has been added to the invoice and will be applied to all items listed before the subtotal or total.

This item is not to be used for an early payment discount.

Payment: Use this item type for partial payments received against invoices.

Sales Tax Item: If you answered the Sales Tax Preference question to the effect that you do charge, collect and remit sales taxes from your clients then you have already set up at least one sales tax item. Review this item to make sure that all the information including the rate and tax authority you make the payment to is correct.

If you collect sales for more than one state or locality than set up a sales tax item for each of them. Some states have multiple sales tax authorities such as the state, county, city and in some cases specific zip codes. Consult your accountant for more information on your requirements.

Sales Tax Group: This item type works similarly to the Group Item type. If you have more than one sales tax item you may want to have your customer invoices only show the total tax being charged instead of listing all the taxes due. Use this item type to accumulate all the appropriate tax rates you need to charge on one invoice line.

Other Lists to Consider

Fixed Asset List

This feature lets you track your fixed assets as you add them to your books. Found under the list menu you can add a new fixed asset by clicking on the Item button at the bottom of the Fixed Asset Item List window and then select New.

Fill in the information including a purchase description, the date purchased and the amount paid.

Choose the account to post this asset to or add a new account to hold this type of asset. You can also note the vendor or payee from whom you purchased the asset, a location of where it will be used should you have the need, reference the purchase order number if one was used for this purchase, the serial number, warranty expiration information and notes.

When the asset is sold you can come back in and record the sales date, sales price and any sales expense incurred.

Use these items when you are preparing a purchase order, or vendor bill or direct payment. This is a way to easily track the purchase of fixed assets and the information your tax preparer will need to determine your depreciation for your tax return.

NOTE: Setting up a Fixed Asset Item will not post a bill, check or purchase order and will not post the purchase amount to the account you have chosen. This item type is used to automatically fill in the information you have provided into a vendor's bill, purchase order or check form when you select it as the item to use.

This feature also does not determine depreciation or post depreciation to your books. It does, however, allow your tax preparer to import this information into the Fixed Asset Manager where this task can be performed saving them time and you money when having your tax return prepared.

The Fixed Asset List is available in all editions, starting with Pro.

Price Levels

Do you have the need to automate the billing of customers at different price levels for the same service or product? This feature will let you do this task easily.

In the Price Level window (found under the List menu) select the Price Level button in the lower left hand corner. Select New.

Name your price level and choose the type you wish to use.

In the per item method, which is only available in Premier or higher editions, you are allowed to set a price level for individual items while the percentage methods sets a price level for all items per customer or job. Select a rounding method from the list provided.

You may assign a price level to specific customers and when you prepare an invoice for those customers the items marked to use price levels (if you chose the per item method) will be automatically used and if your chose the percentage method the price will either be decreased or increased based on how you set up the price level no matter what item(s) you use to populate the invoice.

When preparing the invoice you can click on the rate window and access a pulldown list of price levels that have been set up if you have not marked the customer you are using to use a particular price level or if you wish to change the price level to be used for this invoice.

Billing Rate Levels

Billing rate levels are only available in the Premier Contractor, Professional Services and Accountant editions.

Should you need to bill your customers at different rates for work performed by your employees and vendors, this function automates the process.

Some companies have their personnel perform at different levels of service, resulting in more than one billing rate based on the service provided.

For example, an electrician might bill out at one rate for residential service and another rate for commercial service. Normally you will only be able to bill that one employee at one set rate. This feature allows you to assign more than one rate to a particular employee or vendor.

With the billing rate levels feature you can set either fixed hourly rates or custom hourly rates per service items.

With the fixed hourly rate billing level you will be able use the same hourly rate for all service items performed by people.

Using the custom hourly rate allows you to set a different hourly rate for each service item performed by people with this billing rate.

To use billing rate levels, choose the List menu, then select Billing Rate Level List. In the lower left hand corner click on the Billing Rate Level button and select New to add a new billing rate. Provide a name for this billing rate and choose between the two types of rates.

Choosing the Custom hourly rate level will open a new window where you will see a list of all your service items and their standard rates. Select the service items you wish to assign a billing rate. Either add a billing rate to the column labeled Billing Rate or click on the Adjust Selected Rates button. In this window you will be able to enter a percentage to either lower or increase the standard rate for each service rate you have selected.

Assign the billable rate level to the vendor or employee in their record.

From now on your customers will be billed at the level assigned to the vendor or customer that is assigned to each service item. While vendors and employees can only be assigned one billing level, each type of service they perform can be assigned a different billable rate if you use the custom hour rate level when setting up a new billing rate level.

When you create an invoice you will be given the option to add billable time and other costs to your customer's invoice. When you use a service item in the invoice that has a billable rate attached to it, the billable rate, not the standard rate will be assigned to the invoice.

Sales Tax Codes

Under the List menu select the Sales Tax Codes List to add or edit sales tax codes. In your customer records on the Additional Info tab you can set a default sales tax code for each customer. When you create an invoice or sales receipt in QuickBooks the appropriate tax code will be automatically selected. You can change the tax code in the tax field from the drop down menu which lists all the available codes.

Class List

If you have chosen to use classes set up your class list under the List menu, selecting Class List. At the bottom left hand corner select the Class button to add, edit, or delete classes. Name the class.

You can set up sub-classes if needed and assign a new class to one of the already set up classes.

For example if you are a retail operation with more than one store you might want to set up a class to represent each store. Then set up a sub class for each department in the store.

When posting vendor transactions and customer invoices or sales receipts select the appropriate class on each transaction. You will then be able to run a Profit and Loss statement by class to see a breakdown of each store's department financial effectiveness.

Customer and Vendor Profiles List

Under the List menu you will find the Customer and Vendor Profiles List. Here you can set up one or more of the following custom lists:

Sales Representatives

Customer Types

Vendor Types

Job Types

Terms

Customer Messages

Payment Methods

Ship Via List

Vehicle List

Set up sales reps, customer types, job types, terms, customer messages, payment methods and ship via lists to help you automate invoicing your customers. Once set up your customer records can be set to reflect the information pertinent to a particular customer. Customer Messages can be selected from the invoice form for each sale.

You can also assign vendor types and terms to your vendor records.

Vehicle List

The vehicle list is used to track mileage for individual vehicles.

Set up a vehicle for each vehicle you use for business purposes and then track the mileage used by selecting the Company menu and choosing Enter Vehicle Mileage.

In the new window select the appropriate vehicle from the pull down list and fill in the information as needed. You can choose this to show up in the items to be billed list when you bill your customers by checking the Billable box.

Memorized Transactions

If you have reoccurring transactions you can automate the posting of them. When posting one of these types of transactions whether they may be invoices to clients, vendor bills, sales receipts or sales orders, estimates or purchase orders the process is very similar.

Once the form is filled out and before saving, from the Edit memo select Memorize ****, where the **** represents the name of the form you are using.

Choose the remind me function that you would like, how often this transaction should be processed, the next day the transaction is to be processed.

If you have chosen the Automatically Enter option then the fields Number remaining, and days in advance to enter will be available. Fill in these fields with the needed information.

When you open the database if a memorized transaction is set to process on that date QuickBooks will either remind you to process the transaction or will automatically enter it.

You can edit your Memorized Transactions by going to the List menu and choosing Memorized Transactions List. In the bottom left hand corner click on the Memorized Transaction to edit a transaction that you have first hi lighted in the list.

You can also add a new group, delete a transaction, edit the listing window or print the list.

The next button is titled Enter
Transaction. This button takes you to
the filled out transaction field where you
can post the transaction or edit any of
the fields. Use this function to post the
transaction when you are reminded if
you have not chosen the Enter
Automatically when you set up the
memorized transaction.

199

Entering Your Open Balances

Now is the time to start entering your opening balances. You will need several pieces of information. (See Appendix D) If you are a new company the amount of information you will need to gather up will be less than if you have been in business for a while. In both scenarios you should enlist the aid of your accountant, QuickBooks consultant or bookkeeper.

For a new business, make a list of all assets you are bringing into the business, when those assets where purchased and how much you paid for them. If they have been used by you for personal reasons before being owned by your business you should treat their cost as if you bought used equipment from an unrelated party. In other words what would you pay for them if you were to go buy them today. If you have started a bank account you will need your bank statements. Also if you have billed any clients or incurred any bills or expenses you will need to have those records as well.

With this information in hand you should be all set to begin entering your beginning balances.

If, however, you have been in business for a while, you should also have what is termed a trial balance. This is a list of accounts with their current balances. Depending on the timing of your database set up you may only be entering balance sheet accounts or both balance sheet and income statement accounts. If you are in mid fiscal year then you will be entering both types of account balances. You will also need all the items listed for a new business.

In both cases I would strongly recommend you work with or have the information entered for you by a professional in the bookkeeping or accountant profession.

If you choose to do this yourself, however, this is the procedure. Please note you need to enter these transactions in the exact order as listed.

There are several ways to enter your opening balances and you may use a combination of these methods depending on your data and how much historical data you wish to be able to access.

The first way is through the check register. This is a good way to enter checkbook balances.

If you did not set up a bank account when going through the Start Up Wizard, set up your bank account now and enter your bank balance as it shows on your bank statement.

Use the bank statement that closes one accounting period prior to the opening date of your database.

For example, if you are setting up your database with a January 1st date then use the ending balance as shown on your December 31st bank statement. Post this entry to the "Opening Balance Equity" account. Do not include any checks or deposits that have not cleared your bank statement, you will enter those later.

Next you will be entering your customer and vendor outstanding balances.

You can choose to enter these balances in a lump sum per customer or vendor, or enter individual invoices. If you want to be able to apply payments as they are received or paid out against individual invoices then taking the time to enter individual invoices is the preferred way.

You will need to set up an item to handle these transactions.

Choose the item type non-inventory, name the item "Opening Balance", check the box that states you will be using this item in assemblies or is purchased for a specific customer, and choose the account "Opening Balance Equity" account for both the purchase and sales account fields. Leave the amount fields blank as each entry will be a different sales price or cost.

Go to the Customer or Vendor center, set up the clients or vendors that are needed.

Then either from the Customer or Vendor center, or clicking the icons "Enter Bills", or "Create Invoices" on the home page, start to post the invoices for customers and enter the bills for vendors. You should be entering only those invoices that are outstanding using the original transaction date that should be prior to your start date.

Enter each invoice or bill using the item you created called Opening Balance. Make the date of the bill or invoice you use the same date of the original document. When entering the bills you will have a choice of ways to enter the transaction, Expenses or Item. Choose the Item tab.

Now that you have posted all of your vendor bills and customer invoices, run a Balance Sheet report (Reports, Company & Financial, Balance Sheet Standard). Choose a date that reflects the first day of the month of the start date of your database and check to see that the Accounts Receivable account balance and the Accounts Payable account reflects the amounts owed to you and owed by you as of your start date. If not, then make sure you entered all the invoices and bills that were outstanding and that you used the correct dates when you posted these transactions.

You will need to enter your outstanding balances for Sales Tax by using the Sales Tax Liability account. If you have entered individual customer invoices that included sales tax then do not include those amounts while posting your outstanding sales tax liability as they have already been posted to this account. Determine your outstanding sales tax balance as of the end of the last month prior to your start date, subtract any sales tax posted when you entered your customer's invoices and post the difference to the Sales Tax Liability account using the start date. This amount will only reflect unpaid sales tax for invoices issued prior to your start date that were paid prior to your start date. Review your balance again to verify that the balance showing in your Sales Tax Liability is the amount you owe as of your start date.

Payroll beginning balances and historical data will need to be entered through the Payroll function. You will find a Payroll Setup Wizard under the Employees menu. This wizard will walk you through setting up your company for payroll, entering your employee data, setting up the items needed to track your payroll tax requirements and to enter your year to date data.

Again verify the correct posting of this data by referring to your balance sheet accounts. If you are starting your books beyond the fiscal year start year also check your income statement for accuracy of your payroll and payroll tax expense accounts.

Inventory balances should be posted when you set up your inventory items. At the bottom of each new Inventory or Assembly item you add you will find a section called "Inventory Information". Here you can enter the amount of each inventory part you have on hand, and the total value of that item as of a certain date.

Use the start date you have selected for this date, enter the total number of units you have on hand as of this date and the total value of those units (cost not sales value). Verify the total value of your inventory by reviewing your balance sheet as of the start date.

You can use the General Journal function to enter all other beginning balances. (Company menu, Make General Journals.) This function is a traditional debit and credit entry method. Post all remaining opening balances using the "Opening Balance Equity" account for the offsetting account.

If you chose to enter your Accounts Receivable and/or Accounts Payable balances in a lump sum you can make that entry in the General Journal, however you can only use one of these accounts per entry and the AR or AP account has to be the first account listed in the entry. You will also need a customer or vendor in the Name column. Since you can only use one line in each journal entry for these two accounts you will either need to post the entire AR balance on one line using a pretend customer (ie, Open Balance customer). This is also true for the Accounts Payable balance. If you want to post to each customer or vendor you will need to post a separate entry for each customer and vendor that has an outstanding balance.

If you have been in business prior to setting up your books don't forget to post your Owner's Equity balance as well. This amount would represent previous year net profit/loss.

If you are setting up your books mid-year than post all income and expense account balances that have not already been posted, such as your payroll and payroll tax expenses when you went through the payroll wizard for the current year up to the start of your new database.

If you wish to run monthly or quarterly reports for this year then post each month's ending balances separately using the end of month date for each entry.

Inventory transactions of any type cannot be made using a General Journal entry as there is no way to enter an item. Therefore any transactions made through the General Journal will affect your Inventory account balance but will not adjust the balances of your inventory items which will result in a variance between your account balance and your items balance.

You should now do a final review of your Balance Sheet and if you have posted mid-year income and expenses your Income Statement using the start date you have chosen. Compare these reports to the documents you have supporting your prior year or period balances.

Adding Customers

You can add customers to your database through the Customer Center, or while creating an invoice, sales order, estimate or sales receipt.

The process is the same in all cases. The only difference is that in the Customer Center you select the button labeled "New Customer & Job, and in the various forms you select the "Add New" from the Customer:Job pull down list when populating the form.

When the new customer form opens just fill in the blanks as needed. Start with the customer name. Use this field for either a company name or a person's name. If you are using a person's name you might want to add the last name, comma, then the first name of your customer. This will make it easier to find customers as QuickBooks uses this field to sort your customers on lists and pull down menus.

Do not enter an opening balance here as you will be entering outstanding balances when you post your opening balances. Fill in all the other fields with the information you have (you can always come back later and add information).

On the Additional Info tab you can specify a customer type, payment terms you are assigning this customer, a sales rep, and the preferred method of sending your invoices.

If this customer is one to whom you bill sales tax then fill in the appropriate tax code and tax item. Or provide the resale tax number they have provided you.

You can also select a price level for this customer if you have set up this function.

There are custom fields available for you to add if you wish to have additional information such as birthday dates, spouses name, web address, Sales Region, etc. Click on the Define Fields button, enter the name of the field and check whether you want this field available in any or all the places where these fields can be used - Customer, Vendor, Employee. Once set up in one of these three areas, they are available for use in all of these types of records. These custom fields can also be added to Customer and Vendor forms.

Under the Payment Info tab you add a Customer account number, credit limit and information about their preferred payment method.

If you choose to enter your customer's credit card information remember only those users who have permission to view credit card numbers will be able to see this information.

All of the credit card numbers except the last four will be blocked, however the expiration date and full name and address will be listed.

A user with full access to Accounts Receivable will be able to replace the number with a new one, however. In Enterprise Solutions you have more control over user permissions.

On the Job Info tab you can enter the status of the customer's job (None, Pending, Awarded, In Progress, Closed or Not Awarded), the start date, projected ending date and the actual ending date of the job, a brief job description and job type. You can set up multiple jobs for each customer by selecting Add Job under the New Customer and Job button listed in the Customer Center.

Also found under the New Customer and Job button is the ability to add multiple customers and/or jobs at one time. Choose the Add Multiple Customer:Job selection to access an Excel like spreadsheet where multiple customers and jobs can be entered or cut and pasted from Excel.

When setting up the Excel spreadsheet make sure to order your columns in the same way that your QuickBooks columns are listed in this window. You can add, move or delete columns as necessary by clicking on the Customize Columns button.

When you click on the Save button at the bottom of this window the data you have entered will either set up a new customer or edit a customer already set up with the new information.

This function can be used to add or edit multiple Customer, Vendors, and Service, Inventory Parts and Non-Inventory Parts Items.

Adding Vendors

Adding vendors is very similar to adding customers. Go to the Vendor Center or from the pull down menu of various vendor forms

(Purchase Orders, Receive Inventory, Enter Bills Against Inventory, Enter Bills and Pay Bills). From the Vendor Center select the New Vendor button, New Vendor.

Enter the applicable information as needed. Do not enter the opening balance.

There is a field to enter how the vendor's name should appear on the check should you need this function. The Additional Info tab provides fields to account numbers, vendor type, terms, credit limit and tax id. You should check the box labeled "Vendor eligible for 1099" if appropriate. Check with your accountant for advice on this area.

You also have fields to assign a billing rate level, and to add custom fields. If you have already defined custom fields in the Customer Center or Employee Center and at that time selected to have the Vendor records use those fields as well, those fields will appear here.

On the Account Prefill tab you can set up three accounts to prefill in your forms. If you have check off the "Vendor eligible for 1099" box then make sure the first field listed for this vendor is an account that is assigned to the 1099 category chosen in your 1099 preference setup. You will want to use this account for all payments made to this vendor.

For example if this vendor is a subcontractor and you have assign the account Subcontractor Expenses to the Non-employee Compensation box (#7) in the 1099 preferences, then you want to choose the Subcontractor Expenses account for the first prefill selection.

By selecting a prefill account when posting a vendor transaction this account will automatically be selected when this vendor is used, therefore preventing data entry errors.

What is Next?

You are almost ready to start using QuickBooks. You will want to review all the work you have done already for accuracy and completeness. Now is a great time to perform a backup to preserve what you have already set up. To save your file, choose the File pull down menu, then select Save Copy or Backup. You will be given several backup methods to select from. You can make a backup copy which is a complete copy of your current file. Because this is a large file it is not suitable for emailing your database.

Or you can make a Portable company file which saves the transactional data but removes some non-essential data such as templates, letters, images , etc. This is a great choice should you need to email your CPA or tax-preparer or outside bookkeeper your books as it produces a smaller file but provides all the data.

You can also prepare an Accountant's Copy to send. This type of file allows you to set a date that will allow you to continue working in the future while your accountant can review and make changes or post adjustments dated prior to the date you set.

When your database is returned to you, you will be able to import the changes made to your file without affecting the work you have done while your accountant had your database. In other words, you can both work on the same database at the same time and then have the database reconcile the differences and post the changes when appropriate.

There are some restrictions for the person you sent the file to, but they will be aware of those restrictions and QuickBooks will provide an alert if they attempt to make any changes or adjustments that will not transfer to your file.

The only restriction you will have is the one that doesn't not allow you to post transactions or make any changes or deletions prior to the date you set when preparing the file. This restriction will be removed once you have installed your accountant's changes. You may send this file through your email after preparing it.

Another way to prepare the Accountant's file that you might want to consider is to go to the File menu, select Accountant's Copy Clients Activity and then choose the Save File option. Once the file is saved you can go back to the Client's Activity menu and then select Send to Accountant.

This allows you to set a password and upload your file to Intuit's secure server. Your accountant will receive an email notifying him/her that the file is ready for download. Once downloaded your accountant will be able to open your file and start their review and adjustments. You will have to let your accountant know the password you assigned. This should not be done in the note field that is provided when sending the file but either in a separate email or even better by phoning them. This password should also not be the same password used for the Administrator as you should have set up a user account for your accountant to use with their own

unique user/password log-in for your
file.

At this time, unless you are sending
your file to your QuickBooks consultant
or accountant you should use the
backup option. Click Next.
You are given the option of saving your
file online which is a service Intuit
provides for an additional fee or to a
local backup source. We will choose
the local backup choice. Click Options
to set up where you will save your file.
Select a location to save the file.

Although you can save the file to your computer's hard drive it is always a better choice to save it to a portable hard drive or to a CD or DVD. After all if your computer is no longer useable for any reason, you won't have your database if you have saved it to your local hard drive. Of course it doesn't hurt to save your database to more than one location. Belts and suspenders are always the better solution.

When making your selection you should consider what the backup file will be used for. If you are backing up your database for possible restoring should you database get corrupted then choose a folder that is easy to find should you need it. However if you are preparing this file to send it or deliver it to your accountant then save it to your desktop so you can easily attach it to an email or copy onto a disk. Remember though if sending a file through email is what you want to do you will be better choosing the Portable File option.

If you choose to add the date to the file name you will always have an easy way to determine what is the latest backup. So check this box. You can limit how many backups can be save to the folder you have set up for backups. You will want to have at least 3 backups at any given time. Files occasionally get corrupted in computer land and it doesn't hurt to have an extra file around.

Set up the amount of times you want to open the database before you are reminded to save a new backup.

Generally you want to backup your database whenever you have more new data entered then you feel comfortably recreating should something happen to your database. For some people this means daily, for other weekly or monthly. The rule I always went by was to backup daily if data was being entered on a daily basis. Then I would make a weekly backup. At the end of the month I would make a monthly backup and then either quarterly or yearly. The daily backups would be replaced by the weekly backup at the end of the week, the four to five weeks replaced by a monthly backup, etc. This way I always had a daily, weekly, monthly and yearly backup available for restoring should they be needed. For smaller companies this might be overkill, but the rule of thumb is still "how much data can I recreate and how much data do I want to recreate should something happen to my database?".

Select to have the data completely verified. This takes a bit more time but is worth it. When clicking on the Okay button, if you have selected a location on your local hard drive you will be given a warning and a choice to continue or to select another location. Select the one you wish to do which will bring you back to the screen you saw before you selected the Option button.

Click the Next button. Choose Save It Now. You can also save it now and set up a schedule of future backups or just set up a schedule of future backups.

Click Next. The Save window will open up letting you select a location to save your file in case you wish to change the location you had already chosen. It will default to the location you chose. The file will be automatically named with your company name and the date of the backup. The file will have a .QBB file extension.   Click Save. Your data will be verified and then your backup will be saved.

Ready To Use Your Database

Now you are ready to get down to working with your database.

Design your invoice, estimate, purchase order and letter templates

Under the List menu you will find Templates. Here you will find a list of templates now available to you.

Select the template you wish to customize and click on the Template button in the bottom left corner and choose Edit.

You can edit these templates including choosing what company information is shown.

You can also specify what fields should show on your form (either on screen or printed, or both) including custom fields you have set up, choose footer information, select printing options, and select and add a logo. Select the Additional Customization button at the bottom of the screen to refine your template.

The Layout Designer will allow you to add or delete fields, move fields around and make some format changes to your template.

From the Template List you can also delete, duplicate, import or export and make a template inactive.

Also included are links to online solutions to download predesigned templates and to Create Form Design. In the Create Form Design online tool you will work through a wizard to help you create your own custom designed form template which can be saved and used in QuickBooks.

Form templates and letters can also be customized within the form itself. While using a function that provides you with a form to enter transactional data, select one of the two icons above the Print Preview button. They are labeled Letters (for setting up or editing custom letters using Microsoft Word) and Customize (to customize form templates).

Set Up Budgets and Forecasts functions

Under the Company menu you will find a selection called Planning and Budgeting. Use this function to set up a budget to track budgeted vs actual income and expenditures. You can set up budgets for both Profit and Loss activity and for Balance Sheet accounts.   You can also define the budget to track by class, customer:job or for no additional criteria.

You will be able to choose whether you want to start this budget from the scratch or to use a previous year's actual data. Once you have made these decisions the budget can be adjusted as needed.

On the Reports menu select the Budgets and Forecast to run various comparison reports.

The Forecast feature works in the same manner as the Budget feature but is used for predictions of future activities. You can then run reports to compare actual vs your forecast.

Prepare your Business Plan

Every company no matter how small should have a business plan and QuickBooks helps you perform this task with ease. Select the Use Business Plan Tool found under the Company menu grouped within the Planning and Budgeting selection.

This tool will aid you in preparing a professional and effective business plan for your company.

You can also edit you business plan as your company grows. Don't skip this very important step as banks, investors and others will often ask you for this document. If you already have it ready and up to date, you won't be scrambling when you are asked for it. If you have it readily available you will come across as a professional and well organized business owner.

Review the available reports

QuickBooks provides your company with many, many reports so you can analyze and review your data in many different ways.

You can access the reports either through the Report pull down menu or through the Report Center.

The pull down menu takes you directly to the report you have chosen. The Report Center groups reports by type of activity and displays sample reports with the opportunity to display an enlarged example of the report, select dates, display the report with your data, or favor a particular report.

In the Report Center you will see tabs for Standard, Memorized, Favorite and Recent reports making it an easy way to find the report you are looking for.

The viewing options for the sample reports are Carousel, List or Grid. All the views display sample reports and provide a brief explanation as to the purpose of the report you have selected.

Reports can be modified by clicking on the Modify Report button in the upper left hand corner of the individual report screen.

Modification choices will depend on the report chosen, however most include the ability to choose custom dates, the report basis (cash or accrual), columns to be used, and a sort by selection on the Display Tab.

On the Filters tab you can add or delete fields to be shown on the report. The fields listed will depend on the report selected and will also allow you to select criteria for each field.

On the Header/Footer tab you can choose Header and Footer information to show on the report and select a page layout alignment.

The Fonts and Numbers tab lets you choose a font for various sections of the report and how you wish numbers to appear on your report.

Once you have modified a report you can memorize the report for future use. Click on the Memorize button, name the report and if you wish put it into a group of similar reports. A memorized report can be selected from the Report menu under the Memorized Reports selection or from the Reports Center within the Memorized tab.

For most companies the standard reports provided by QuickBooks will be all they need. However for others the ability to export reports out to Excel and to other report writers will enable them to customize their reports to give them more sophisticated analysis tools.

QuickBooks also has a Financial Statement Designer tool available (Included with Enterprise solution, available for an additional cost for Pro and Premier). This tool provides customization of financial statements with many features for the user.

Check out the new Company Snapshot feature

New in 2009 QuickBooks now has a Company Snapshot feature. The icon is located right next to your Home page icon. Click on this icon to access many graphical representations of what is happening in your business. From year to year comparisons of Income and Expenses, lists of your account balances and customers who owe you money to an expense breakdown on the Company tab.

On the Payment tab access a Receivable report listing, an accounts receivable aging chart, and recent customer transactions.

You can also access QuickLinks to many of the daily tasks such as receiving payments, creating invoices or sales receipts, create credits and refunds, create estimates and make deposits. You can also Pay Bills, get reminders and search for transactions.

Drill down to reports or original transactions by double clicking on a line item or chart section.

That is just the tip of the iceberg. Click on Add Content to Your Company Snapshot to add more charts. There are nineteen different charts available. Each tab has different types of charts to add to your snapshot windows.

Users will only be able to view those charts that are associated with the areas they have been given permission to access.

So much information, presented in an easy way to view all on one page.

You can make this page your Home page by opening the Company Snapshot and then selecting the preference (Edit, preferences) for Desktop. Click the My Preference tab and then choose Save current desktop. Uncheck the option that says Show Home page when opening company file. Click OK.

The snapshot page is user dependent. If you make changes or select to have it your home page, only your log in will display those changes.

Mission Accomplished

You have now completed the initial set up process and are ready to start using QuickBooks to post your daily financial transactions. Properly set up your QuickBooks database will provide you with the information you need to run your business efficiently. You now have reports available that will allow you to analyze your business, aiding you in your decisions as your business needs change and grow.

Congratulations on a job well done and for taking the task of your business financial health seriously.

Appendix A:

New Features in 2011

The Company Snapshot page now includes a tab for customer information. Customer Snapshot gives you a consolidated view so you can assess at a glance your customer's purchase history, average days to pay, and outstanding balance and make timely decisions on customer requests. You can also identify your top customers by revenue and payment consistency, and prioritize them accordingly.

You can now invoice multiple customers at once with Batch Invoicing.

QuickBooks search can locate any account, report or invoice. Enter a keyword and all related reports, invoices, contacts and transactions will appear.

There is a new Collections Center identifying overdue or almost due invoices and email out notices from Outlook, Yahoo, Gmail or HotMail accounts.

Complete transactions faster with convenient access to your customer or vendor's balance and transaction history.

Send invoices and estimates out from QuickBooks using your Yahoo, Gmail, or Hotmail account.

Keep track of vendors' remittances address with the new field added to the vendor record.

Mark invoices paid with the Paid Date Stamp.

And free 1 hour phone session with one of Intuit's QuickBooks Experts.

Added in 2010 and available in 2011:

Add or edit multiple entries from one spreadsheet view.

Auto sign checks

Create professional looking invoices & forms

Added in 2009 and available in 2010 and 2011:

Easily find customer, vendor & items with

QuickFilter

Track international sales and expenses

Run reports and backup data while others work in the same company file

Customize your Company Snapshot

Instantly communicate with others with QuickBooks Messenger

Added in 2008 and available in 2009, 2010 and 2011

Create email estimates, invoices and reports

Allow multiple users to work in
QuickBooks at the same time

Download transactions from your
financial institution

Manage payroll and track key tax dates
in the Payroll Center

Get a quick view to key data with the
Customer, Vendor and Employee
Centers

Get insights to make better decisions
from the new re-designed Report
Center

Import from prior versions of QuickBooks

Allow accountants to review historical data while you work.

Appendix B:

List of QuickBooks
File Extensions

As you work with QuickBooks you will see several types of files listed. They are as follows:

.DES	Template Form
.IFF	Interchange Format File
.ND	Network Data File
.QBA	Accountant's Working File

.QBA.TLG Log	Accountant's File
.QBB	Backup File
.QBM	Portable Company File
.QBR	Report Template File
.QBW	QuickBooks for Windows File
.QBW.TLG	Transaction Log File
.QBX	Accountant's Copy (Export File)
.QBY	Accountant's Copy (Import File)

The ones you will most often refer to are the QBB, QBM, QBW, QBX and QBY files.

The QBB and QBM files are used when you either prepare a backup file or save a portable file.
The QBW is your every day working file.

The QBX file is the file you prepare and send to your accountant so they may work on your file and you may continue to work in your file at the same time. You set a date that you cannot work prior to and your accountant cannot work beyond at the time you prepare this file. The QBY file is the file your accountant sends back to you after making whatever adjustments were made. From this file you will be able to import the adjustments made without overriding the work you have done.

Appendix C:

Subcontractor vs an Employee

You may be thinking that someone is a subcontractor because you pay them by a check or cash without withholding payroll taxes. But that is not how the IRS sees it. According to the Internal Revenue Service an employee is defined as anyone who performs a service that is subject to the will and control of an employer. If you are laying down the rules as to what will be done and how it is to be done, then you have an employer/employee relationship and must by law withhold income taxes.

Now there are many business owners that do not understand this and risk penalties and fines as well as being responsible for your "employee's" non withheld income taxes, social security and Medicare taxes. This can add up to a large amount of money. So if your business is one which often uses subcontractors, you might want to review your policies in this area. The government often conducts "employee audits" within industries that fall into this category.

So what is an employee audit? The IRS will send in an agent to review your payroll records and subcontractor payments. Persons being paid as subcontractors could be reclassified as employees if they do not meet certain requirements. Some, but by no means all, of the criteria the agent will be looking for are as follows:

Does the subcontractor only work for you – or do they have other clients?

Do they provide their own tools, work space?

Do they set their own hours?

Is the work they perform, how and when it is done determined by them?

Do they have a business phone, business cards, and printed billing forms?

Do they have a legitimate place of business (a real office for example)?

Do they advertise?

Do they have employees being paid as employees?

Do they have business insurance?

Ignoring this risk may seem the easiest and most cost effective way to do business, but if you are audited, you will wish you had followed the rules. If you think you might be in a gray area, then give your accountant a call so they may review your situation and make recommendations. For more information see the IRS Article at www.irs.gov "Independent Contractors vs. Employees."

Appendix D:

Information to Gather

☐ Company information such as FID and State ID numbers, type of entity, type of tax form filed.

☐ Your fiscal year ending date

☐ Prior Year Tax Return or Trial Balance

☐ Prior month Bank Statement including a list of uncleared deposits and checks

☐ List of unpaid customer invoices as of the start date of your database.

☐ List of unpaid vendor invoices as of the start date of your database

☐ Year to date payroll data, taxes owed, individual employee records including checks issued, workmen's compensation data, payroll tax agencies information, etc.

☐ Sales tax data including ID number(s), agencies to remit to, tax liability due date, and balances owed as of the start date of your database.

☐ A current inventory list including cost values, descriptions, ID numbers if used,

☐ Vendors names, addresses, contact info, and FID numbers.

☐ Customer names, addresses and contact info

☐ Any other information you need to set up all the features and functions listed in this book.

Appendix E:

Chart of Accounts Numbering Schemes and Parent vs Sub-Accounts

Numbers are used in a Chart of Accounts to sort the accounts correctly. Also, between you and me, accountants are much better at remembering numbers than they are at names so they prefer numbers. When using numbers, each segment is assigned a specific group of numbers. Typically these are as follows:

- Assets – 1,000's

- Liabilities - 2,000's

- Equity - 3,000's

- Income - 4,000's

- Cost of Goods Sold - 5,000's

- Marketing & Promotion Expenses – 6,000's

- General & Administrative – 7,000's

- Other Income - 8,000's

- Other Expense - 9,000's

When a Sales Expense segment is used it is assigned the 6000 range and each of the remaining segments move up a range. Leave room between sub-segments so you will be able to add if needed. When setting up numbers within a segment make sure you leave some room between each account as you may also want to add accounts.

Sometimes you may want to group a set of accounts to have them appear as one category on a financial statement instead of each account being listed separately. An example of this is when you have several cash type accounts such as checking, savings, money market, etc. Should you want all of these accounts to appear on your balance sheet summarized on one line then set up a parent account and then assign each individual account as a sub account of the parent.

This is easily done by creating a new account, in this example one named Cash and Cash Equivalents. Then edit each account to be included in this parent account by assigning them to the parent account. Select the checkbox under the account name and choose the parent account. Note: Only accounts within the same type can be assigned to a parent account of the same type. You cannot assign a Bank account type account to an Other Asset type parent account for example.

Sub accounts can also act as parent accounts for even more customization of your financial statements.

To prevent users from accidentally posting to a parent account in the Preference Accounting on the Company tab, select Use Account Numbers and check off Show Lowest SubAccount Only. Even if you are not using account numbers do this as you won't have the ability to set this function otherwise. You do not have to use numbers if you have chosen the Use Account Numbers selection.

23073683R00168

Made in the USA
San Bernardino, CA
20 January 2019